MW01626815
This book
belongs to...

# A QUICK NOTE FROM US...

Thank you for your purchase! If you enjoyed this book, then please leave feedback! If you have any enquiries or want to send us a selfie with this book, then email at ben@bclesterbooks.com

Is this book misprinted? Email us and we will sort out a replacement copy.

**Please note: Items beginning with Q, U and X are rare with regards to a child's vocabulary for this age range, so are excluded.**

**Visit us at www.bclesterbooks.com for more!**

I SPY WITH MY LITTLE EYE
SOMETHING BEGINNING WITH...
A
COUNTRIES

A
IS FOR
AUSTRALIA

I SPY WITH MY LITTLE EYE
SOMETHING BEGINNING WITH...
B
LANDMARKS

# B IS FOR BIG BEN

# I SPY WITH MY LITTLE EYE SOMETHING BEGINNING WITH... C

RELIGIONS

C IS FOR CHRISTIANITY

I SPY WITH MY LITTLE EYE
SOMETHING BEGINNING WITH...
D
SEA ANIMALS

# D IS FOR DOLPHIN

I SPY WITH MY LITTLE EYE
SOMETHING BEGINNING WITH...
E
中国
COUNTRIES

# E IS FOR EGYPT

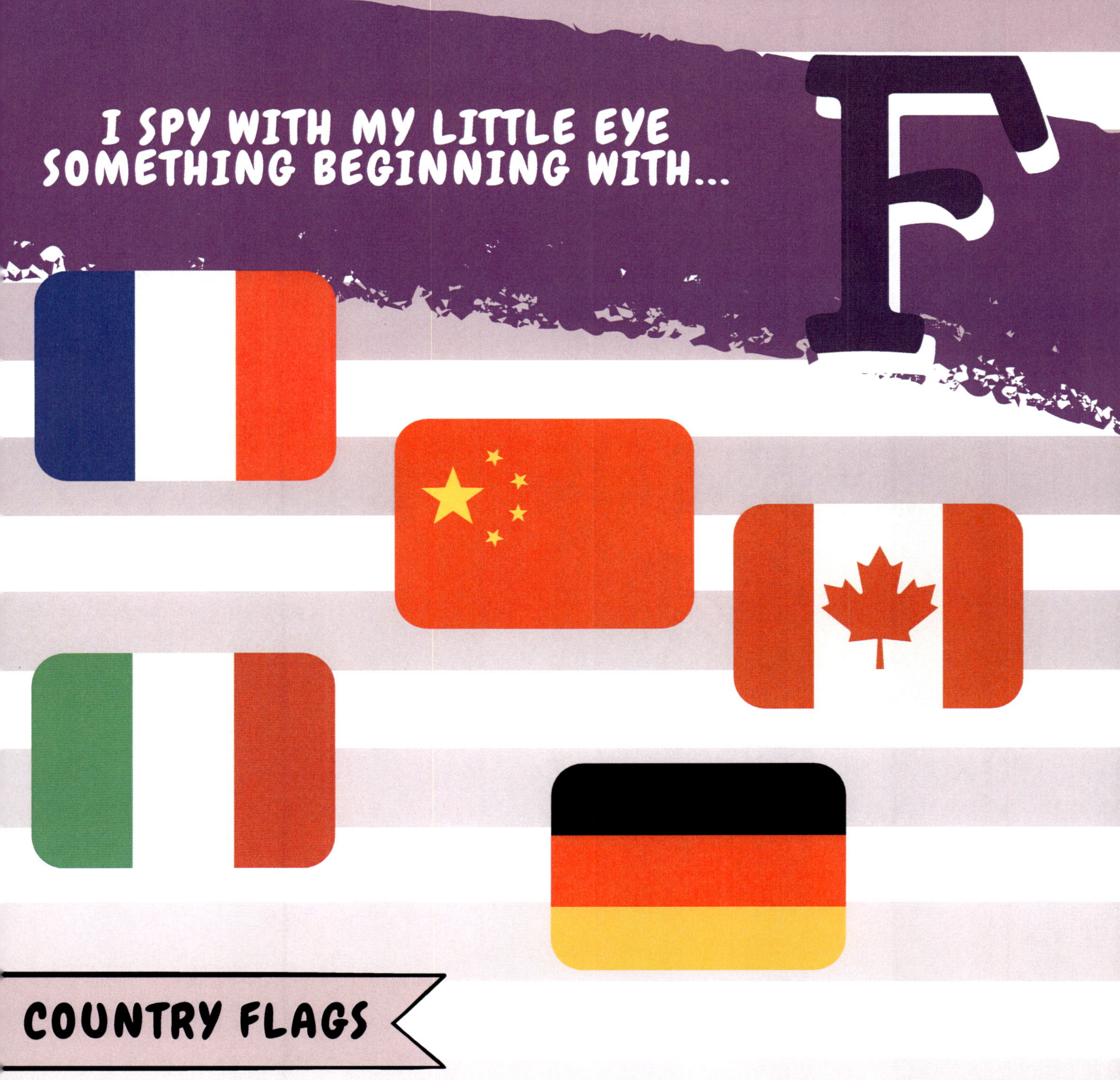
I SPY WITH MY LITTLE EYE
SOMETHING BEGINNING WITH...
F
COUNTRY FLAGS

# F IS FOR FRANCE

# I SPY WITH MY LITTLE EYE SOMETHING BEGINNING WITH... G

LANDMARKS

G
IS FOR
GREAT WALL OF
CHINA

CITY BUILDINGS

H
IS FOR
HOSPITAL

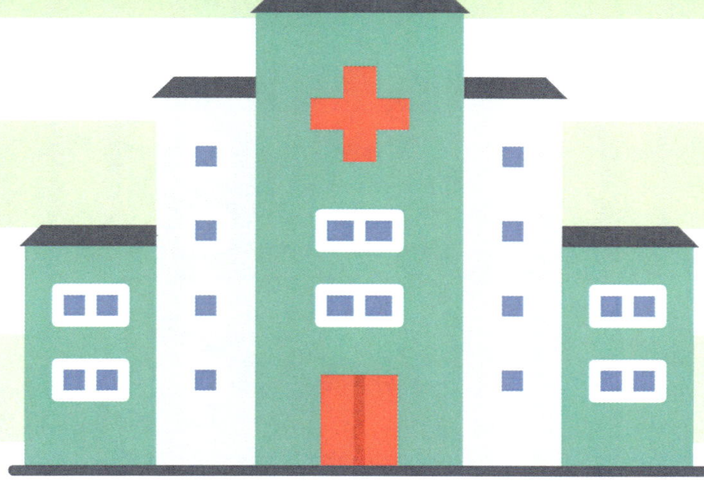

I SPY WITH MY LITTLE EYE
SOMETHING BEGINNING WITH...

# I

HABITATION

# I IS FOR IGLOO

# J

COUNTRY FLAGS

# J IS FOR JAPAN

I SPY WITH MY LITTLE EYE
SOMETHING BEGINNING WITH...
K
ANIMALS

K
IS FOR
KANGAROO

I SPY WITH MY LITTLE EYE
SOMETHING BEGINNING WITH...
L
OUTDOORS

L
IS FOR
LEAVES

I SPY WITH MY LITTLE EYE
SOMETHING BEGINNING WITH...
M
LANDFORMS

M
IS FOR
MOUNTAIN

I SPY WITH MY LITTLE EYE
SOMETHING BEGINNING WITH...
N
WORLD FOODS

# N IS FOR NOODLES

I SPY WITH MY LITTLE EYE
SOMETHING BEGINNING WITH...
O
IN THE OCEAN

O
IS FOR
OCTOPUS

I SPY WITH MY LITTLE EYE
SOMETHING BEGINNING WITH...
P
ON THE BEACH

# P IS FOR PALM TREE

I SPY WITH MY LITTLE EYE
SOMETHING BEGINNING WITH...
R
RUSSIA
ITALY
UK
USA
CHINA
CAPITAL CITIES

ITALY

I SPY WITH MY LITTLE EYE
SOMETHING BEGINNING WITH...
S
WEATHER

# S IS FOR SUNNY

I SPY WITH MY LITTLE EYE
SOMETHING BEGINNING WITH...
T
TRANSPORT

# IS FOR TRAIN

I SPY WITH MY LITTLE EYE
SOMETHING BEGINNING WITH...
V
NATURAL DISASTERS

# IS FOR VOLCANO

I SPY WITH MY LITTLE EYE
SOMETHING BEGINNING
WITH...
W
LANDFORMS

W IS FOR WATERFALL

I SPY WITH MY LITTLE EYE SOMETHING BEGINNING WITH... Y

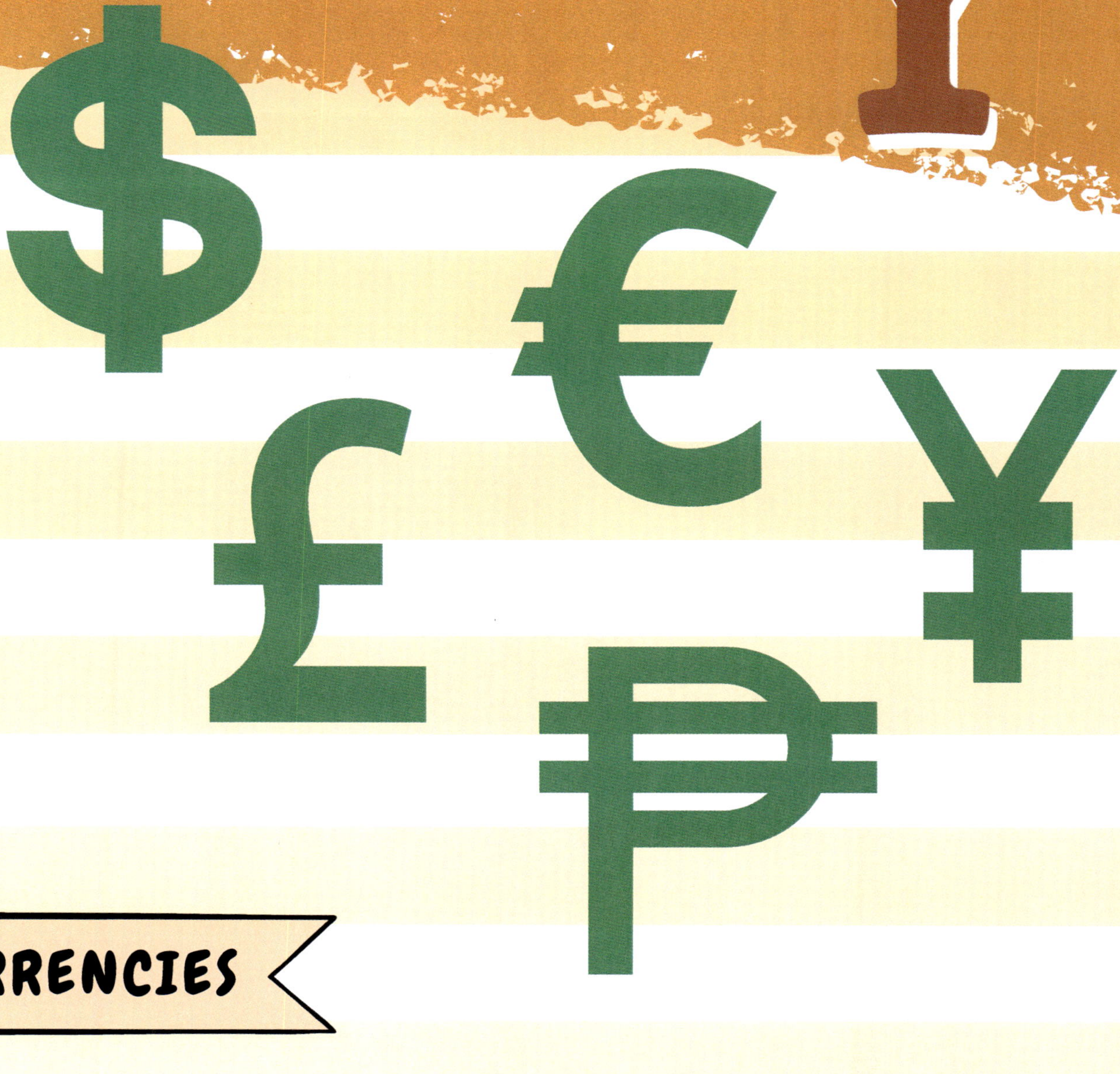

CURRENCIES

# Y IS FOR YEN

SAFARI ANIMALS

# Z IS FOR ZEBRA

Made in the USA
Las Vegas, NV
15 October 2023

79158480R00031